MW00416461

To _____

From _____

Other giftbooks in the same series by Helen Exley:
Missing You …   Bon Voyage
Sisters …   When Love is Forever
True Love …   For a Good Friend

Published simultaneously in 1996 by Exley Publications in Great Britain, and
Exley Giftbooks in the USA.
Copyright © Helen Exley 1996

12 11 10 9 8 7 6 5 4 3 2 1

Border illustrations by Juliette Clarke
Edited and pictures selected by Helen Exley

ISBN 1-85015-795-2

A copy of the CIP data is available from the British Library on request. All
rights reserved. No part of this publication may be reproduced or transmitted
in any form or by any means, electronic or mechanical, including photocopy,
recording or any information storage and retrieval system without permission
in writing from the Publisher.

Designed by Pinpoint Design.
Picture research by Image Select, London.
Typeset by Delta, Watford.
Printed in Singapore

Exley Publications Ltd, 16 Chalk Hill, Watford, Herts. WD1 4BN.
Exley Giftbooks, 232 Madison Avenue, Suite 1206, NY 10016, USA.

Bon Appétit!

QUOTATIONS SELECTED BY *Helen* EXLEY

NEW YORK · WATFORD, UK

Laughter is brightest where food is best.

IRISH PROVERB

A good cook is like a sorceress who dispenses happiness.

ELSA SCHIAPARELLI
(1890-1973)

The discovery of a new dish does more for the happiness of the human race than the discovery of a star.

ANTHELME BRILLAT-SAVARIN
(1775-1826)

Real cooking is an art form. A gift to be shared.

OPRAH WINFREY,
FROM *"IN THE KITCHEN WITH ROSIE"*

I believe that the truly dedicated cook has food in
her mind, or at least on the periphery of it, at all
times. As a poet unconsciously earmarks a word that
rhymes handily with another, or as a painter
mentally notes a tint of a shade of a color that spells
dawn, so the food-minded person sniffs an out-of-
the-way herb....

PEG BRACKEN, b.1920

The preparation of good food is merely another
expression of art, one of the joys of civilized living....

DIONE LUCAS (1909-1971)

*C*ooking is like love. It should be entered into with abandon or not at all.

HARRIET VAN HORNE, b.1920

The only real stumbling block is fear of failure. In cooking you've got to have a what-the-hell attitude.

JULIA CHILD, b.1912

I like a cook who smiles out loud when he tastes his own work. Let God worry about your modesty; I want to see your enthusiasm.

ROBERT FARRAR CAPON, b.1925

[Cooking] calls for a light head, a generous
spirit, and a large heart.

PAUL GAUGUIN (1848-1903)

Some people's food always tastes better than
others, even if they are cooking the same
dish at the same dinner. Now I will tell you
why – because one person has more life in
them – more fire, more vitality, more guts –
than others. A person without these things
can never make food taste right, no matter
what materials you give them, it is no use...
You have got to throw feeling into cooking.

ROSA LEWIS

WELCOME!

Small cheer and great welcome makes a merry feast.

WILLIAM SHAKESPEARE (1564-1616)

... because of this incredible operation where we give the best of ourselves, planning, selecting, preparing, even improvising a last-minute extra treat, because of the excitement and the delight in sharing delicious things, everyone forgets differences and old feuds.

MIREILLE JOHNSTON,
FROM *"EDUCATING A PALATE"*

Of soup and love, the first is best.

SPANISH PROVERB

The angels in Paradise eat nothing but
vermicelli al pomidoro.

DUKE OF BOVINO

Sex is good, but not as good as fresh sweet
corn.

GARRISON KEILLOR, b.1942

The olive tree is surely the richest gift in
Heaven. I can scarcely expect bread.

THOMAS JEFFERSON (1743-1826)

Garlic is as good as ten mothers.

LES BLANK

Mayonnaise: One of the sauces which serve
the French in place of a state religion.

AMBROSE BIERCE (1842-1914)

When one has tasted watermelons one
knows what angels eat.

MARK TWAIN (1835-1910)

Wish I had time for just one more bowl of
chilli.

THE DYING WORDS OF KIT CARSON
(1809-1868)

One cannot think well, love well, sleep well,
if one has not dined well.

VIRGINIA WOOLF (1882-1941)
FROM *"A ROOM OF ONE'S OWN"*

Food... can look beautiful, taste exquisite,
smell wonderful, make people feel good,
bring them together, inspire romantic
feelings, help them to share things.

ROSAMOND RICHARDSON,
FROM *"SEASONAL PLEASURES"*

A good meal soothes the soul as it
regenerates the body. From the abundance of
it flows a benign benevolence.

FREDERICK W. HACKWOOD,
FROM *"GOOD CHEER"*

PURE WICKED LUST!

Huge blond *babas, Mont Blancs* snowy with whipped cream, cakes
speckled with white almonds and green pistachio nuts, hillocks of
chocolate-covered pastry....

GIUSEPPE DI LAMPEDUSA

O, blackberry tart, with berries as big as your thumb, purple and
black, and thick with juice, and a crust to endear them that will go
to cream in your mouth, and both passing down with such a taste
that will make you close your eyes and wish you might live forever
in the wideness of that rich moment.

RICHARD LLEWELLYN (1907-1983)

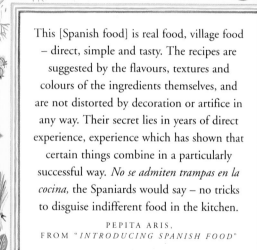

This [Spanish food] is real food, village food – direct, simple and tasty. The recipes are suggested by the flavours, textures and colours of the ingredients themselves, and are not distorted by decoration or artifice in any way. Their secret lies in years of direct experience, experience which has shown that certain things combine in a particularly successful way. *No se admiten trampas en la cocina,* the Spaniards would say – no tricks to disguise indifferent food in the kitchen.

PEPITA ARIS,
FROM "*INTRODUCING SPANISH FOOD*"

They make their pride in making their
dinner cost much; I make my pride in
making my dinner cost little.

HENRY DAVID THOREAU (1817-1862)

... an honest laborious Country-man,
with good Bread, Salt and a little Parsley,
will make a contented Meal with a
roasted Onion.

JOHN EVELYN (1620-1706)

... kitchens should be thought of as the centre of the house. They need above all space for talking, playing, bringing up children, sewing, having a meal, reading, sitting and thinking. One may have to walk about a bit, but where's the harm in that? Everything will not be ship-shape, galley-fashion, but it's in this kind of place that good food has flourished. It's from this secret retreat that the exploration of man's curious and close relationship with food, beyond the point of nourishment can start.

JANE GRIGSON, FROM *"GOOD THINGS"*

COOKING WITH LOVE

The most indispensable ingredient of all
good home cooking: love for those you are
cooking for.

SOPHIA LOREN, b.1934

Cooking with love means never having to
feel chained to your stove, never feeling that
getting dinner on the table is a teeth-gritting
experience rather than a charming interlude.

FRANCIS ANTHONY

Jewish cuisine differs from that of my father's in both philosophy and content, but in its preoccupation with food as a gesture of love, the two have much in common. If the price we pay for that gesture be a little pain in the night, a little agony on the bathroom scales, a prowl down dark corridors groping for the Bisodol [antacid] – well, who said love was all roses without a thorn?

RUSSELL BAKER

The glowing hearth shoots beams of light into all corners, cuts out great shadows on the ceiling, casts a fresh rose tint on the blue faience, and makes the fantastic edifice of pans glow like a wall of fire.... "This kitchen is a world and this chimney is the sun."

VICTOR HUGO (1802-1885)

SIMPLICITY

Good cooking is honest, sincere and simple.

ELIZABETH DAVID,
FROM *"FRENCH COUNTRY COOKING"*

Cuisine is when things taste like themselves.

CURNONSKY

He who distinguishes the true savor of his
food can never be a glutton; he who does
not cannot be otherwise.

HENRY DAVID THOREAU (1817-1862)

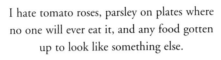

I hate tomato roses, parsley on plates where
no one will ever eat it, and any food gotten
up to look like something else.

BARBARA KAFKA

Cook things so you can tell what they are.
Good plain food ain't committed no crime
an' don't need no disguise. Fancified cooks is
the criminals.

MARY LASSWELL (1905-1994)

Everything tastes better outdoors.

CLAUDIA RODEN, FROM "*PICNIC*"

*Seating themselves on the greensward, they
eat while the corks fly and there is talk,
laughter and merriment, and perfect
freedom, for the universe is their drawing
room and the sun their lamp. Besides, they
have appetite, Nature's special gift, which
lends to such a meal a vivacity unknown
indoors, however beautiful the surroundings.*

ANTHELME BRILLAT-SAVARIN
(1775-1826)

It is the aroma that fills the space between the plate and your head. In the *apparent* emptiness wafts most of the real art of cooking. Just hold your nose and eat and you'll see how vital aromas are!

GRAHAM KERR

Pounding fragrant things – particularly garlic, basil, parsley – is a tremendous antidote to depression. But it applies also to juniper berries, coriander seeds and the grilled fruits of the chili pepper. Pounding these things produces an alteration in one's being – from sighing with fatigue to inhaling with pleasure.

PATIENCE GRAY

The smell of good bread baking, like the sound of lightly flowing water, is indescribable in its evocation of innocence and delight.

...

[Breadmaking is] one of those almost hypnotic businesses, like a dance from some ancient ceremony. It leaves you filled with peace, and the house filled with one of the world's sweetest smells... there is no chiropractic treatment, no Yoga exercise, no hour of meditation in a music-throbbing chapel, that will leave you emptier of bad thoughts than this homely ceremony of making bread.

M.F.K. FISHER (1908-1992),
FROM *"THE ART OF EATING"*

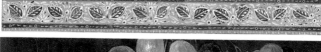

It was in France that I first learned about food. And that even the selection of a perfect pear, a ripe piece of brie, the freshest butter, the highest quality cream, were as important as the way the dish you were going to be served was actually cooked.

ROBERT CARRIER

I KNOW THE COMFORT...

*I know the look of an apple that is roasting
and sizzling on the hearth on a winter's
evening, and I know the comfort that comes
of eating it hot, along with some sugar and a
drench of cream.... I know how the nuts
taken in conjunction with winter apples,
cider, and doughnuts, make old people's tales
and old jokes sound fresh and crisp and
enchanting.*

MARK TWAIN (1835-1910)

The smell of buttered toast simply talked to Toad, and with no uncertain voice; talked of warm kitchens, of breakfasts on bright frosty mornings, of cosy parlour firesides on winter evenings, when one's ramble was over and slippered feet were propped on the fender; of the purring of contented cats, and twitter of sleepy canaries.

KENNETH GRAHAME (1859-1932)

Bread is the warmest, kindest of words. Write it always with a capital letter, like your own name.

RUSSIAN CAFE SIGN

Bread deals with living things, with giving life, with growth, with the seed, the grain that nurtures. It is not coincidence that we say bread is the staff of life.

LIONEL POILANE

When there is very little else left to believe in, one can still believe in an honest loaf of fragrant, home-baked bread.

ANNA THOMAS, b.1948

 Bread, milk and butter are of venerable antiquity. The taste of the morning of the world.

LEIGH HUNT (1784-1859)

HOME COOKING

*We all have hometown appetites.
Every other person is a bundle of longing for
the simplicities of good taste once enjoyed on
the farm or in the hometown [he or she]
left behind.*

CLEMENTINE PADDLEFORD

*What is patriotism but the love of the food one
ate as a child?*

LIN YUTANG (1895-1976)

... it looks as if the new "green" mood, the fashion for old houses, traditional kitchens and regional produce, might be a way of rescuing the art of cooking. We're discovering that it's not so much a question of digging out our grandmothers' recipes, of recalling the unrivalled flavour of the food we had as children, as a question of reasserting our identity, indeed of conserving our birthright. Nowadays, with European bureaucrats threatening cultural homogenization, cooking is a way of affirming our differences. When we're faced with the invasion by McDonald's, it becomes a form of resistance.

BENOITE GROULT, FROM "LA MER A LA CUISINE" IN *"LOAVES AND WISHES"*

What is a feast? A feast is an occasion where food, friends and drinks are harmoniously celebrated, no matter how humble or grand the occasion....

KEITH FLOYD, b.1943,
FROM *"A FEAST OF FLOYD"*

*They eat, they drink, and in communion sweet
Quaff immortality and joy.*

JOHN MILTON (1606-1674)

There is a communion of more than our bodies when bread is broken and wine drunk.

M.F.K. FISHER (1908-1992),
FROM *"THE ART OF EATING"*

It [nouvelle cuisine] is often rather unkindly
called a little bit of nothing on a big white
plate.

FROM *"THE FINE ART OF FOOD"*

ON NOUVELLE CUISINE: It's so beautifully
arranged on the plate – you know someone's
fingers have been all over it.

JULIA CHILD, b.1912

Life is too short to stuff a mushroom.

SHIRLEY CONRAN, b.1932,
FROM *"SUPERWOMAN"*

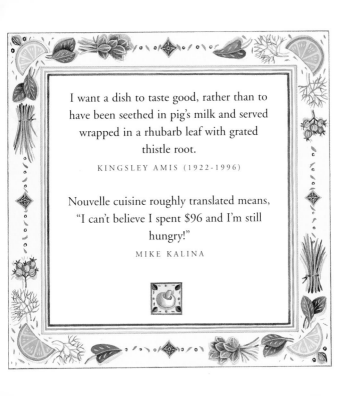

I want a dish to taste good, rather than to have been seethed in pig's milk and served wrapped in a rhubarb leaf with grated thistle root.

KINGSLEY AMIS (1922-1996)

Nouvelle cuisine roughly translated means, "I can't believe I spent $96 and I'm still hungry!"

MIKE KALINA

Shopping for food is one of the most exciting things. Whether you are sifting spices through your fingers in Istanbul, haggling... in a Portuguese market, waltzing through Harrods' Food Hall, arguing with storeholders in a Provençal market, shopping in a Leeds market or pushing a trolley through Waitrose. Shopping is not only exciting, it's also very important.... Imagine that it is as important as any other of your activities: like having your hair done, choosing tickets for the theatre, or planning your holiday and take the same trouble over it.

KEITH FLOYD, b.1943,
FROM *"A FEAST OF FLOYD"*

I am a gourmet
YOU are a gourmand
HE is fat.

CRAIG BROWN,
FROM *"THE TIMES"*, NOVEMBER 1989

I have never been anything so refined as a
gourmet; so I am happy to say that I am still
quite capable of being a glutton.
My ignorance of cookery is such that I can
even eat the food in the most fashionable
and expensive hotels in London.
G. K. CHESTERTON (1874-1936)

After eating, an *epicure* gives a thin smile of satisfaction; a *gastronome,* burping into his napkin, praises the food in a magazine; a *gourmet* repressing his burp, criticizes the food in the same magazine, a *gourmand* belches happily and tells everybody where he ate; a *glutton* embraces the white porcelain altar, or, more plainly, he barfs.

WILLIAM SAFIRE

Gourmand: a glutton, gormand, bellie-god, greedie-gut; a great eater, monstrous feeder, gully-gut.

RANDLE COTGRAVE,
FROM *"A DICTIONARIE OF THE FRENCH
AND ENGLISH TONGUES"*, 1611

It seems to me that our three basic needs, for food and security and love, are so mixed and mingled and entwined that we cannot straightly think of one without the others. So it happens that when I write of hunger, I am really writing about love and the hunger for it, and warmth and the love of it and the hunger for it... and then the warmth and richness and fine reality of hunger satisfied... and it is all one.

M.F.K. FISHER (1908-1992),
FROM *"THE ART OF EATING"*

WITH FRIENDS

While the pot boils, friendship blooms.
A.B. CHEALES

Men that can have a communication in nothing else can sympathetically eat together, can still rise into some glow of brotherhood over food and wine.
THOMAS CARLYLE (1795-1881)

The gentle art of gastronomy is a friendly one. It hurdles the language barrier, makes friends among civilized people, and warms the heart.
SAMUEL CHAMBERLAIN

PLATES OF SUNSHINE...

Cooking is an art and patience a virtue. Patience is an essential attribute for all good cooks; patience, and the all-important ability to shop first and then decide on the dish to cook, which will depend on season, price, availability, and so on. These are the hallmarks of a successful and practical cook. There is no mystery. Careful shopping, fresh ingredients and an unhurried approach are nearly all you need.

There is one more thing – love. Love for food and love for those you invite to your table. With a combination of these things you can be an artist – not perhaps in the representational style of a Dutch master, but rather more like Gauguin, the naive, or Van Gogh, the impressionist. Plates or pictures of sunshine taste of happiness and love.

KEITH FLOYD, b.1943,
FROM *"A FEAST OF FLOYD"*

REMEMBERING

Even the simplest meal can be so much more than its parts, a wealth of pleasures so indelible that it can be recalled, even after decades, as fresh as if it happened yesterday. Why, when we forget so much else, should this be so? Appetite surely sharpens the senses, refines the sensual appreciation of sight, smell and taste.

CLAIRE CLIFTON AND COLIN SPENCER,
FROM "*THE FABER BOOK OF FOOD*"

One remembers flavor more than dates and times in the memory portion of the brain. Taste and smell and grandma's rolling the dough... that's it!

JEFF SMITH (THE FRUGAL GOURMET)

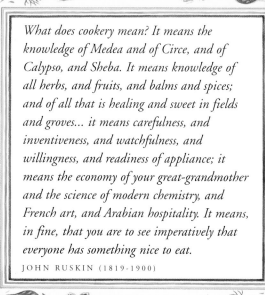

What does cookery mean? It means the knowledge of Medea and of Circe, and of Calypso, and Sheba. It means knowledge of all herbs, and fruits, and balms and spices; and of all that is healing and sweet in fields and groves... it means carefulness, and inventiveness, and watchfulness, and willingness, and readiness of appliance; it means the economy of your great-grandmother and the science of modern chemistry, and French art, and Arabian hospitality. It means, in fine, that you are to see imperatively that everyone has something nice to eat.

JOHN RUSKIN (1819-1900)

My kitchen is a mystical place, a kind of temple for me. It is a place where the surfaces seem to have significance, where the sounds and odors carry meaning that transfers from the past and bridges to the future.

PEARL BAILEY (1918-1990)

No matter where I take my guests, it seems they like my kitchen best.

PENNSYLVANIA DUTCH SAYING

Acknowledgements: The publishers are grateful for permission to reproduce copyright material. Whilst every effort has been made to trace copyright holders, the publishers would be pleased to hear any not here acknowledged. KEITH FLOYD: Extracts from *A Feast of Floyd,* reprinted by permission of HarperCollins*Publishers* UK, © Keith Floyd, 1989. Extract from *Floyd on France,* reprinted by permission of BBC Books, © Keith Floyd, 1987.

Picture Credits: Exley Publications is very grateful to the following individuals and organizations for permission to reproduce their pictures: Bridgeman Art Library (BAL), Fine Art Photographic Library (FAP), Index, Scala (SCA), Statenskonst Museer, Stockholm (SKM). Cover: main picture: Paul Cezanne, *Still life with teapot,* BAL, background picture: © 1996 Brenda Evans, *All Aflame,* BAL; title page: Jose Lopez Enguidanos, *Watermelon and Figs,* Index; page 6: Hanna Pauli, *Frukostdags,* SKM; page 9: William B